Whc

Rock

What Is
Rock and Roll?

by Jim O'Connor

illustrated by Gregory Copeland

Penguin Workshop
An Imprint of Penguin Random House

To Jane A., who stole my heart at the Fillmore East
(by going into the wrong bathroom)—JOC

To my multitalented brother, Tim—GC

PENGUIN WORKSHOP
Penguin Young Readers Group
An Imprint of Penguin Random House LLC

Library of Congress Cataloging-in-Publication Data is available.

ISBN 9780451533814 (paperback)   10 9 8 7 6 5 4 3 2 1
ISBN 9780451533838 (library binding)   10 9 8 7 6 5 4 3 2 1

Contents

What Is Rock and Roll? 1

The Roots of Rock 3

The Motown Sound 12

The Beatles 24

The Beach Boys 38

Acid Rock 44

Sounds of the '70s 60

A Kid from New Jersey 71

Grunge 78

The King of Pop 86

Into the Future 94

Timelines 102

Bibliography 104

What Is Rock and Roll?

In August of 1953, an eighteen-year-old truck driver walked into a small building in Memphis, Tennessee. The neon signs in the windows read "Memphis Recording Service."

The young man was named Elvis Presley. He wanted to record two songs, "My Happiness" and "That's When Your Heartaches Begin," as a birthday present for his mother. The receptionist, Marion Keisker, was also the sound engineer that day. So she led Elvis into the studio and put him in front of the microphone.

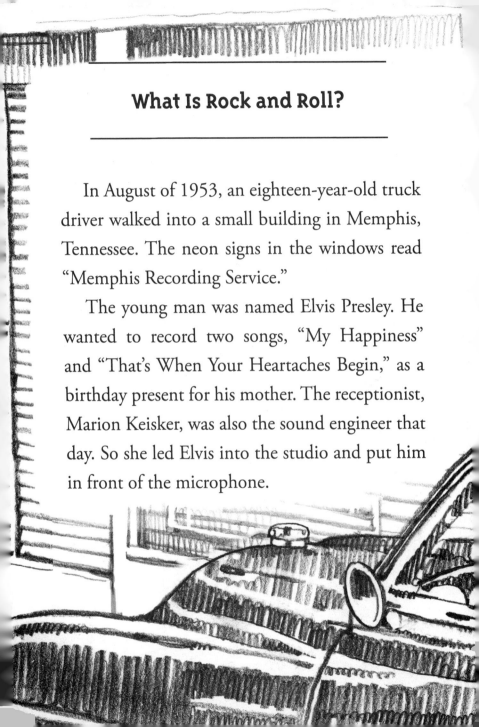

Then she went into the tiny control room and recorded what he sang.

There was something about the yearning quality in Elvis Presley's voice that intrigued her. So she decided to make a copy for her boss, Sam Phillips, to hear.

That was the beginning of Elvis Presley's career.

It was also a breakthrough for rock and roll.

Sam Phillips

CHAPTER 1
The Roots of Rock

Rock and roll is true made-in-the-USA music. But in the early 1950s, if you asked kids what rock music was, most of them wouldn't have had a clue what you were talking about.

Rock music didn't just spring up one day out of nowhere. Its sound owes a lot to the rhythm and blues (R&B) music of the 1940s and '50s.

Rhythm and blues was the popular music of black Americans. The songs were exciting, with a strong, insistent beat. R&B music was completely different from what was played on radio stations for white audiences. Those stations played a mix of big band, jazz, and silly pop hits like "Doggie in the Window." The music was safe and parent friendly.

Then white performers began covering popular black songs. ("Covering" means doing a new version of an older song.) Elvis Presley had a huge hit with "Hound Dog." It had first been recorded by a black singer named Big Mama Thornton in 1952.

Big Mama Thornton

Elvis rocketed to stardom in the mid-1950s. In large part he owed his success to a man named Sam Phillips. Sam grew up very poor in Florence, Alabama. He was white. But as a young boy he picked cotton in the fields alongside black laborers who sang while they worked. Sam loved their music.

Sam later moved to Memphis, Tennessee. There he opened a recording studio and started his own record company—Sun Records. He signed up many African American performers. Sam wanted to bring their music to white audiences.

Sam also let amateurs, black and white, record in his tiny studio. That's how Elvis Presley got started. Sam believed Elvis had a special talent.

So Sam got two musicians he knew, guitar player Scotty Moore and bassist Bill Black, to back up the young singer.

Often producers recorded a song in one or two takes. (A "take" is a single complete recording of a song.) This kept costs low. But Sam believed that singers—most of all, new singers—needed time to get it right. He would record the same song, or parts of a song, over and over.

Sam did the same thing with Elvis.

In 1954, Sam Phillips recorded Elvis, Scotty, and Bill playing the old blues song "That's All Right" and a speeded-up cover of the country music classic "Blue Moon of Kentucky."

Country Music

Rock music was also influenced by country music. Country music began as far back as the late 1700s, when colonists came to America from England and Scotland. Their music took root in the South in poor white communities. Some country songs are slow, sad ballads about lost love and hard times. But others are lighthearted, fast-paced, and great to dance to. Dolly Parton is the most famous country music singer of modern times.

On August 5, 1954, Elvis performed the songs at an outdoor concert in Memphis. The show sold out. Neither Elvis nor his bandmates had ever been in front of such a huge crowd. They were very nervous.

In fact, Elvis was so nervous, his legs kept shaking and twitching while he sang. The crowd thought it was part of the act. Girls started screaming with excitement.

After that, Elvis kept on shaking and swinging his hips at every performance. Teenagers loved it, but their parents hated it.

Elvis went on to become the biggest rock star in the world. He had twenty-eight number-one singles and ten number-one albums. John Lennon of the Beatles once said, "Before Elvis there was nothing." After Elvis, rock and roll was here to stay.

Guitars

The sound of an electric guitar is at the heart of rock and roll. The two most iconic electric guitars are the Fender Stratocaster and the Gibson Les Paul.

Rock guitarists love them because they are loud, versatile, and cool looking.

In 1954, Leo Fender introduced the Stratocaster. It had three pickups—devices that converted the vibrations of the strings into an electrical signal.

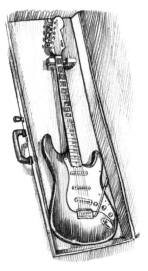

Les Paul designed his solid body electric at the same time. He was already a famous guitar player, so Gibson, the manufacturer, named the guitar after him. Today, many musicians own and play both Fenders and Les Pauls in concert.

Les Paul playing his Gibson

CHAPTER 2
The Motown Sound

In the early '60s, R&B became known as "soul music." By this time, all kids, black and white, listened to it and danced to it. Soul music was hugely popular.

Sometimes soul music was light and fun, as when the Supremes, a girl-group trio, sang "Baby Love."

Sometimes soul music had a strong gospel flavor. Gospel songs came from African American churches. They were known for having a "call and response" pattern where the lead singer presented a question and other singers gave a reply.

Aretha Franklin became known as the Queen of Soul. She started singing in church when she was a little girl growing up in Detroit, Michigan. Her soul hit "Think" is a great example of a call-and-response song. In it, Aretha is warning  her boyfriend that he'd better think before he goes out with another girl. The backup group keeps repeating "Think!" which reinforces Aretha's warning and also propels the song along.

Three record companies ruled soul music— Motown, Atlantic, and Stax.

Motown was founded in 1959 by Berry Gordy in his hometown of Detroit. Because Detroit was the center of the US car industry, many people called it the Motor City. Berry shortened the name to Motown.

Berry Gordy outside the Motown offices

Motown songs often had a fast pop feel. The Motown sound went beyond the simple guitars and drums of R&B and early rock hits. It used tambourines to accent the back beat, "strings" like violins and cellos, and "horns" (saxophones and trumpets). Berry Gordy said the key to hits was the KISS Principle, which meant "Keep It Simple, Stupid."

Berry's formula worked. Motown had many of the biggest groups of the soul era. Three of them—the Supremes, the Temptations, and Smokey Robinson and the Miracles—were hometown success stories. They had all grown up in Detroit. Other superstars of Motown included Stevie Wonder and the Jackson Five—the group where Michael Jackson started out as the six-year-old lead singer.

The Jackson Five

Records

In the 1960s, LP (long-playing) records usually had twelve songs or "cuts"—six on one side and six on the other. Often a song on an LP album would also be released as a "45"—a much smaller record with a big hole in the center. The 45s were the most popular records for teenagers in the 1950s and 1960s. Why? There was only one song per side, so they were very cheap. Side A had the song that the record company thought would be more popular than the Side B song. DJs at radio stations were told to play Side A songs.

Radios

In those early days of rock, the only way to hear music if you were outdoors was to listen to a car radio. That changed when transistor radios were developed. They were small enough to fit in a pocket. They were powered by a small nine-volt battery and weighed less than a pound. Although the radio's small speaker produced a tinny sound, the popularity of rock and roll helped sell billions of transistor radios during the '60s and '70s. Today, original transistor radios are valuable collector items.

Motown groups always had great singers, great arrangements, and great outfits. The girl groups, like the Supremes, all wore the same glamorous dresses. The guy groups were just as sharp, with matching suits and shoes. And while they sang, the groups would move their feet and hands in unison. It was thrilling to watch.

Stax Records, located in Memphis, competed with Motown. It called itself "Soulsville USA." Many Stax groups had a sound that was very close to gospel music. The recording studio was an old movie theater. The space gave the music recorded there a deep, churchlike sound.

Stax's biggest star was Otis Redding. Redding had a powerful, haunting voice that could express joy or despair. His last recording, "Sittin' on the Dock of the Bay," was his finest. It's about a lonely man who has moved far away from home. Sadly, not long after recording what became his biggest hit, Otis Redding died in a

Otis Redding

plane crash. He was only twenty-six years old.

Sam and Dave were a powerful Stax soul duo known for their high-energy shows. They were nicknamed the Sultans of Sweat because they would soak through their fancy red, white, or green suits at every show.

Sam and Dave had ten hits, one right after another. They included "Hold On, I'm Comin'," "Soul Man," and "When Something Is Wrong with My Baby." Unfortunately, these incredible

performers never got along. They broke up several times and finally called it quits for good in 1981.

Atlantic Records was started in New York and grew into a powerhouse company. One of its founders was Ahmet Ertegun, a man with an incredible gift for spotting great new talent. Atlantic's music sounded better because of the way it was recorded.

Stereo Sound

For many years, all music was recorded in "mono." This meant that all the instruments and voices were heard as one channel of sound. (Back then a record player usually only had one speaker.) Atlantic was the first record company to record in stereophonic (stereo) sound. This divided the music onto two channels. Part of the band might be on the right channel and the rest on the left one. The sound from the two speakers mixed together resulted in a much bigger, fuller sound.

Atlantic had great success with soul groups such as the Drifters, the Coasters, and the singer Ben E. King. Aretha Franklin was the label's biggest star. But by the mid-1960s, soul was becoming a smaller part of Atlantic's business.

Atlantic had signed on hard rock groups like the Rolling Stones. Motown moved to Los Angeles. Its greatest days were over. And Stax was no longer the hit factory it had once been.

Why did soul lose popularity?

It was because of four young men from England with floppy hair. Their rock songs made their way across the Atlantic Ocean and became instant hits in the USA.

It was the start of the British Invasion of rock and roll.

1960s Dance Crazes

Half the fun of early rock-and-roll music was dancing to it. Soon songs started coming out that started brand-new dances. Probably the most famous—and also the first—was "The Twist," by Chubby Checker. Everybody was doing the Twist—

even grown-ups. Soon other dance crazes followed, each one based a song. There was the Mashed Potato from a song called "Mashed Potato Time," as well as the Watusi, the Pony, and the Loco-Motion. Every weekday afternoon, kids could watch teenagers doing these dances on the TV show *American Bandstand.*

CHAPTER 3
The Beatles

A revolution in rock music started in Liverpool, England, when teenagers John Lennon, Paul McCartney, and George Harrison formed a band. They called themselves the Silver Beatles.

All three played guitar. They added a close friend, Stu Sutcliffe, on bass guitar, and drummer Pete Best to the band.

The group couldn't find club jobs in England. So, in 1960, they went to Hamburg, Germany, where they were hired as the house band in a bar. They played nearly every night, which turned them into a very tight band. They soon shortened their name to the Beatles.

In April 1962, Stu Sutcliffe died suddenly, and Paul replaced him on bass. At that point, the group had a smart manager named Brian Epstein.

Brian Epstein

John, Paul, and George knew by then that Pete Best was not a strong enough drummer. So that August, Brian Epstein fired Pete. The group got another guy from Liverpool, Ringo Starr, to take his place. Brian told the Beatles to dress alike, in suits that often had no collars. They had new haircuts, too.

Ringo Starr

Hair

When the Beatles first got to Hamburg, they dressed in black leather jackets and wore their hair with a big wave in front. The sides were combed back and formed a "duck tail." Lots of pop musicians, including Elvis Presley, had similar haircuts.

Then Stu's girlfriend asked him to change his hairstyle. He grew his hair long enough to cover the tops of his ears. And he combed his hair down over his forehead. The rest of the band laughed at Stu's new look. But eventually George, Paul, and John got similar haircuts—what became known as "the Beatle cut."

Stu Sutcliffe

"Beatlemania" struck England on January 11, 1963, when "Please Please Me" was released as a single and became an instant hit. Early Beatles songs had a strong beat and simple lyrics about teen

love, with catchy choruses and great harmonies.

Beatles concerts got crazy. Girls screamed. Some fainted from excitement. There hadn't been anything like it since Elvis.

In February of 1964, the Beatles had their first US tour. As soon as they got off the airplane in New York City, a horde of screaming fans greeted them. They also appeared on a popular Sunday-night TV show called *The Ed Sullivan Show*. It

was the first time many American teenagers saw the group perform.

The Beatles were in their late teens and early twenties when they wrote their first songs like "She Loves You." With its simple, repeated chorus

of "yeah, yeah, yeah," it sounds like it was written and sung by teenagers. It's peppy, fun, simple, and great to dance to.

Then, in December 1965, the Beatles released *Rubber Soul.* This was a completely different kind of Beatles album—the music was far more complex. If you play "She Loves You" and then play "In My Life" from *Rubber Soul,* you will hear the difference. "In My Life" is a great song, full of feeling. In it, someone is remembering all the people and places he's loved in the past.

The sound of the music in *Rubber Soul* was different, too. Songs featured unusual

A sitar

instruments: an Indian stringed instrument called a sitar, a piano altered to sound like a harpsichord, and a distorted fuzz bass guitar.

In June of 1967, the Beatles' most famous album was released— *Sgt. Pepper's Lonely Hearts Club Band*. It had thirteen songs on it, including "When

I'm Sixty-Four," "Lucy in the Sky with Diamonds," and the title song. No two songs sounded alike.

As they had grown more famous, however, problems among the Beatles grew bigger. In the beginning, John and Paul wrote nearly all the Beatles' songs. George, however, was also a talented songwriter. But only one or two of his songs seemed to make it onto an album. That made him angry.

Then, in 1967, their manager, Brian Epstein, died, and the band lost the glue that held them together. Epstein had acted as a go-between and peacemaker during fights.

John's romance with the artist Yoko Ono created more conflict. John insisted on having her sit in on all recording sessions. He wanted her advice. This made the other Beatles furious. They had always had an agreement that no wives or girlfriends could come to the studio when they were working.

Yoko Ono

All the problems came to a head in April 1970: Paul announced he was releasing a solo album. The Beatles were breaking up. It caught fans by surprise and made headlines in newspapers around the world.

In later years, all of the Beatles would have successful solo careers, but their breakup meant the end of an amazing chapter in rock music.

Tragedy

On December 8, 1980, in New York City, John Lennon was shot to death by a mentally ill "fan" seeking fame. It happened right in front of the apartment building where he lived with Yoko Ono and their young son. Lennon was only forty years old. The following Sunday, a crowd of 225,000 people gathered for ten minutes of silence in Central Park. In October 1985, a memorial to John Lennon, called Strawberry Fields, was opened in Central Park. It is a tribute to Lennon and a reference to one of his famous songs.

The British Invasion

After the Beatles, almost any band from England became overnight sensations in the United States. This was called "the British Invasion" by the press. The group that became most famous was the Rolling Stones, with Mick Jagger as lead singer. They had longer, scruffier hair than the Beatles and didn't wear matching suits. Also, they looked like "bad boys." One newspaper article asked "Would You Let Your Daughter Marry a Rolling Stone?" For most parents, the answer was no.

Besides the Rolling Stones, other British groups such as the Who and the Kinks had real musical talent and went on to have long successful careers. Others, however, got by on English accents and stale, music-hall songs like "Mrs. Brown You've Got a Lovely Daughter" (Herman's Hermits) or "Do the Freddy" (Freddy and the Dreamers).

The Rolling Stones

CHAPTER 4
The Beach Boys

A very different band grew up at the same time as the Beatles. Their music came out of Southern California, with its beaches and sunny skies. The band was made up of three brothers—Brian, Dennis, and Carl Wilson—their cousin Mike Love, and a high-school friend, Al Jardine. They called themselves the Beach Boys.

The Beach Boys' early songs were about the California teen lifestyle—surfing, driving cool cars, and dating pretty girls.

Their first single, "Surfin'," was a big hit in the Los Angeles area, followed soon after by "409," a song named for Chevrolet's high-powered engine.

The original Beach Boys

Brian Wilson was the creative force behind the Beach Boys' music and lyrics. But Brian had grown tired of writing bland pop hits. The band's mix of guitars and drums was too simple for his taste. So Brian stopped touring. While the Beach Boys were on the road, he had time to try out new things in music.

When he heard *Rubber Soul*, Brian understood that the Beatles were changing the sound and structure of rock music. Rock changed from music that was great to dance to into music that you simply listened to. Brian wanted to compete with the Beatles' latest albums. Soon he began experimenting with non-pop instruments like violins and cellos, piccolos, and even xylophones, sleigh bells, empty Coke cans, and barking dogs.

The result of all the time Brian spent playing around with music was an album called *Pet Sounds*. The other Beach Boys sang vocals but did not play any instruments on it. Instead, Brian recorded it with a crew of top studio musicians.

All the songs on *Pet Sounds* are linked with a common theme—loneliness. And although the album had disappointing sales when it came out, it did produce several big single hits, including "Caroline, No," "God Only Knows," and "Wouldn't It Be Nice."

Even before *Pet Sounds* was in stores, the Beatles heard it. The musician who replaced Brian on tour had come to London. He brought a copy of *Pet Sounds* for John and Paul to listen to. As soon as the record was finished

playing, they asked to hear it again. They had never experienced anything like it. They wanted to make their next album even better than Brian Wilson's masterpiece.

In June of 1967, the Beatles released *Sgt. Pepper's Lonely Hearts Club Band.* Which album was better? That depends on whom you ask. In 2003, *Rolling Stone* magazine put together a list of the "500 Greatest Rock Albums." *Pet Sounds* came in at number two and *Sgt. Pepper* was number one.

As for Brian, he began work on a new album called *Smile*. But he was struggling with drug problems and mental illness. He did not put his life back together until 1995. After that he finally finished *Smile*.

In the meantime, the Beach Boys continued without him for several years, playing the old surfing and hot-rod songs. The Beach Boys left their mark on rock and roll, but by the late 1960s, their glory days were over.

CHAPTER 5
Acid Rock

The late 1960s were a troubling time in the United States. Many young people no longer believed in the way of life that their parents led. Calling themselves "hippies," they rejected war and violence and greed. Some tried to expand their minds by using illegal drugs such as marijuana or LSD, which was known as acid.

Rock and roll reflected the times. Psychedelic or acid rock often tried to copy the mind-expanding effects of LSD.

In the United States, the center of acid rock was Haight-Ashbury, a run-down neighborhood in San Francisco, California. Many psychedelic bands lived together there—the Grateful Dead, Jefferson Airplane, Quicksilver Messenger Service, and Big Brother and the Holding Company.

On many of these groups' albums, there were long instrumentals (music without words) that were called "jams." In concert, one song might last twenty minutes, like "Dark Star" by the Grateful Dead.

The Grateful Dead

Heavily distorted guitars that used "wah-wah pedals" and "fuzz boxes" were also part of the music. Many psychedelic bands also used organs, harpsichords, or early synthesizers to create a floating, pulsating undercurrent that made the music feel otherworldly. Very often at concerts, light shows would be projected onto a screen above and behind the band. Swirling shapes changed color and size as the music played.

The lyrics to some acid-rock songs seemed to make no sense. Here are words to a song by a group called the 13th Floor Elevators. "Bedouin tribes ascending, from the egg into the  flower, alpha information sending . . ." What does that mean? Your guess is as good as anybody's.

Psychedelic influences appeared in the art on posters and album covers. Super-bright colors and swirling lettering forced viewers to look long and hard at posters for concerts at the Fillmore West in San Francisco and other places.

The first major hippie music festival, Monterey Pop, was held in 1967 in Monterey, California. Thirty thousand fans filled the fairgrounds. A new singer, Janis Joplin, with the band Big Brother and the Holding Company, stunned the crowd with a raw, piercing song called "Ball and Chain."

The Who appeared. They were famous in England but almost unknown in the United States. Their showstopping finale was "My Generation," with its memorable line "I hope I die before I get old." As the song ended, guitarist Pete Townshend smashed his Stratocaster guitar and amplifier, smoke bombs exploded, and Keith Moon kicked his drum set to pieces.

A trio called the Jimi Hendrix Experience was next. Hendrix had not wanted to follow the Who because he knew they stole every show. However, he had lost a coin toss with Pete Townshend and had to go on after the Who.

Jimi Hendrix was black and from the United States. But he was a hard rocker and not in any way like the soul musicians of the early '60s. Jimi was left-handed but played his right-handed Fender Stratocaster reversed and upside down. His trio, the Jimi Hendrix Experience, started out in England. Hendrix was a star over there before he became one in his home country.

At Monterey Pop, Jimi Hendrix proved that he owned any stage he performed on. He used distortion and feedback on his guitar as if they were separate instruments. Jimi finished the set with the song "Wild Thing." He played his Stratocaster with his teeth and also behind his head.

Other Sounds of the '60s

At pretty much the same time that acid rock flourished, softer, sweeter music also became popular. It was called folk rock. It took old folk songs, then added electric guitar, some tambourines, and harmonica to make a new sound. Listen to the Byrds' cover of Bob Dylan's "Mr. Tambourine Man" and "My Back Pages."

The Byrds

Country rock used some country music instruments, like the pedal-steel guitar, mandolin, and fiddle. Gram Parsons, who was briefly in the Byrds, is often credited with getting country rock started with a band called the Flying Burrito Brothers. He was an exceptionally gifted songwriter whose career was cut short by a drug overdose in 1973. He was twenty-six.

Gram Parsons

At the end, Hendrix knelt on the stage and set his guitar on fire. He then smashed it to pieces and threw them into the audience.

Jimi Hendrix was also the last act at the most famous rock festival ever held. It took place in

August 1969 in Bethel, New York. It was called Woodstock and was advertised as "Three Days of Peace and Music." It drew four hundred thousand young people from all around the United States to see thirty-two music acts, including Santana, Creedence Clearwater Revival, Jefferson Airplane, and the Grateful Dead. There were heavy rains that turned the large area in front of the stage into a sea of mud. Fans got drenched but stayed for the music and did their best to have a wonderful time.

At nine o'clock on Sunday morning, Hendrix and his band took the stage. By then the crowd had shrunk to between thirty and forty thousand people.

Near the end of his set, Hendrix played a feedback-drenched version of "The Star-Spangled Banner." He re-created the roar of cannons and the bursting of shells. Jimi wore a red bandanna and a white fringed jacket with blue beads: the colors of the American flag.

In years to come, there would be other, larger music festivals in many places around the world. But Woodstock was a landmark.

Guitar Gods

Jimi Hendrix is probably the guitar player that everyone else wants to be. But there are other greats who also are referred to as guitar gods.

Chuck Berry was one of the pioneers of rock guitar. John Lennon once said, "If you tried to give rock and roll another name, you might call it Chuck Berry."

Chuck Berry

Prince was such an exciting performer with such a distinctive look that sometimes his guitar-playing could be overlooked. Watching him play can make your jaw drop.

Eric Clapton

Eric Clapton's playing seems effortless even when he is tearing off a super-fast string of notes.

The Allman Brothers Band had not one but two outstanding guitar players. Dickey Betts and Duane Allman could play long, complicated solos—even in unison!

Jeff Beck has been in many bands and can play any style of music—the blues, jazz fusion, rockabilly, as well as solid rock.

Jeff Beck

CHAPTER 6
Sounds of the '70s

The year 1970 was very sad for fans of rock music. Besides the April breakup of the Beatles, Jimi Hendrix died in September after combining alcohol with drugs. In October, Janis Joplin, who was recording with a new band, also died of a heroin overdose. Nine months after that, Jim Morrison, lead singer of the acid-rock group the Doors, died of heart failure. It had been brought on by alcohol and heroin. All three were only twenty-seven years old.

Was this the end of rock and roll?

Jim Morrison

Hardly. There were new sounds to be heard.

Disco music became hot in the 1970s. It was smooth music with a steady, repeating beat. People danced to disco all night long at clubs called discotheques.

Then came punk rock. Punk was a loud, angry rebellion against the repetitive beats of disco and the long, complicated, and overproduced "hippie" songs of the late '60s. Many punk rockers wanted to get back to a simple, hard-pounding sound that was more like the rock and roll of early days. The songs often had three chord progressions and simple lyrics, and they were usually short—often not even three minutes long.

Punk rock took off in the United States in part because of CBGB, a New York City rock-and-roll club that opened in 1973. CBGB was a place for punk bands to play their music live, to an audience of rock fans.

One of the most popular American punk bands, the Ramones, played CBGB for the first time in 1974. Although none of them were related, these four friends from Queens, New York, adopted "Ramone" as their common last name. They got the idea from Paul McCartney, a member of the

Beatles. Paul used the name "Paul Ramon" when he checked in to hotels, so people wouldn't know he was staying there.

Joey Ramone was the lead singer. Johnny Ramone played guitar. Dee Dee Ramone played bass guitar and wrote many of the songs. Tommy Ramone was the drummer until 1977; he was followed by Marky Ramone. Some of the Ramones' most well-known songs were "Blitzkrieg Bop," "I Wanna Be Sedated," and "Rock 'n' Roll High School."

Besides the sound of their music, the Ramones had the "punk look": skinny ripped jeans, ratty T-shirts, beat-up sneakers, and black leather motorcycle jackets.

In their early days, Ramones concerts were often messy. One club owner said that a forty-minute set was twenty minutes of music and twenty minutes of the band arguing with one another. In time, however, they got their act

together and toured for over twenty years, playing more than two thousand concerts. Although they never had a major hit record, the Ramones had a devoted following of fans. They also made a huge impact on other bands of the era, as well as on a younger generation of rock musicians, like Green Day, Black Flag, and Red Hot Chili Peppers.

Blondie was another hard-driving '70s New York City punk band that got its start playing at CBGB. The lead singer, Debbie Harry, had a killer rock voice and a tough-girl attitude that was perfect for songs like "Rip Her to Shreds" and "One Way or Another." Blondie continues to record new music and tour, after more than forty years.

Blondie took punk rock and mixed it with other styles of music, like pop. This created something new, called New Wave.

The Talking Heads were another New Wave band. They played their first show at CBGB as the Ramones' opening act. Most songs were written by the Talking Heads' leader David Byrne—songs such as "Psycho Killer," "Once in a Lifetime," and "Burning Down the House" that are still often heard on rock radio stations today.

During the 1970s, glam rock (also known as glitter rock) was born in England, then found fans in the United States. Glam bands often wore fancy costumes, stage makeup, and high platform boots.

Glam rock's biggest star was David Bowie. In 1972, Bowie released his concept album, *The Rise and Fall of Ziggy Stardust and His Spiders from Mars.* A "concept album" is a collection of songs

that are all about one theme. Sometimes concept albums tell stories. The songs on *Ziggy Stardust* tell a story about an alien named Ziggy who comes to Earth and becomes a rock star. Bowie's band wore high shiny black boots and multicolor jumpsuits. David as Ziggy dyed his hair bright red, wore pale white makeup, and dressed in silver suits. The first single from the album, "Starman," became a hit.

Bowie went on to act in movies, like *Labyrinth* and *The Man Who Fell to Earth*. He also painted and recorded many more albums. *Let's Dance* came out in 1984. It included three giant hits: the album's title song, "China Girl," and "Modern Love." Bowie was a rock giant and a major influence on many different types of rock, including punk and grunge. His final album, *Blackstar*, was released two days before his death in 2016.

CHAPTER 7
A Kid from New Jersey

David Bowie was British through and through. However, in the 1970s, a homegrown, "Born in the U.S.A." superstar was coming into his own as an incredible singer and songwriter. He was a kid from New Jersey. His name was Bruce Springsteen.

In high school, he played in several local bands and was nicknamed "the Boss" because he was a natural leader. Over time Bruce met the musicians who would become famous as the E Street Band. (The group got its name because it rehearsed at a house on E Street in Belmar, New Jersey. They were the backup band for Bruce Springsteen for many years.)

Bruce and the band played many shows at a club called the Stone Pony in Asbury Park, New Jersey. Bruce's manager got him to audition at the

office of John Hammond of Columbia Records. Hammond loved what he heard but wanted to see Bruce perform that night in front of a live audience at a New York City club called the Gaslight. Hammond was impressed with Bruce's show. He signed him up with Columbia Records.

Springsteen's first two albums didn't sell well. But in 1975, *Born to Run* made Bruce a star. In time, the album sold six million copies, and its title track became a hit single.

Bruce Springsteen's songs, with their thumping beat, show his New Jersey roots. He writes about the struggles that ordinary, working-class people face, trying to find love, success, and happiness. His songs are almost like stories, and many have strong messages. For example, his hit "Born in the U.S.A." was about the hard times facing US soldiers coming home from a far-off war in Vietnam. He also wrote about American factories closing down and putting people out of work.

When he performed, Bruce didn't wear fancy stage costumes or look like a hippie. He preferred well-worn blue jeans, T-shirts, and a leather jacket. Almost every show was a high energy three-hour performance that left Bruce, the band, and the audience elated and exhausted at the same time.

After forty years, Bruce Springsteen is still recording great albums and touring. Long after Elvis, long after the Beatles, long after Janis Joplin, there is still Bruce Springsteen.

Beyond Records and Radios

In the late 1960s, the cassette tape and cassette player appeared. Instead of an LP record, fans could buy a tape with all the songs on a group's album.  Or they could purchase a blank tape and record songs from different groups.

At first, cassette players were big and bulky. Sony changed that. It brought out the Walkman tape player in 1979. It was small and light and had great sound. Millions were sold.

But by the early 1990s, listening to cassette tapes was a thing of the past.

They were pushed aside by the CD, or compact disc. Small, round, and thin, the CD had much better sound than vinyl records or tapes.

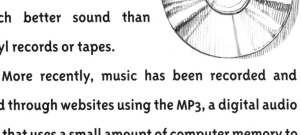

More recently, music has been recorded and sold through websites using the MP3, a digital audio file that uses a small amount of computer memory to record a song or an album.

Interestingly, some music fans don't care for the "perfect" sound of MP3s. They prefer playing old-time vinyl records with their more "real" sound. Once again, sales of vinyl albums are way up. There's a saying and it's true: Everything old is new again.

CHAPTER 8
Grunge

The city of Seattle, Washington, was never considered a rock capital, not like Detroit had been in the 1960s with soul music. That changed in the late '80s and early '90s, when "grunge" bands from Seattle brought a new sound to rock music.

It was guitar driven and heavy, with a little punk mixed in. Grunge rock sounded raw and unrehearsed, as if a bunch of friends in a garage were playing just for fun. And grunge had its own look—flannel shirts, long underwear, combat boots, T-shirts, jeans, and big droopy sweaters.

The record company Sub Pop brought the sounds of Seattle to a wider audience. Soundgarden and Mudhoney were two of Sub Pop's earliest and most successful grunge bands.

Grunge music truly exploded when the band Nirvana released its second album, *Nevermind*, in 1991. It hit #1 on the Billboard album chart and went on to sell thirty million copies worldwide.

Kurt Cobain was the lead singer-songwriter-guitarist for Nirvana. His songs often mixed melodic verses with screaming choruses. Nirvana's hit single "Smells Like Teen Spirit" captures the band's power.

Nirvana

But the sudden success was hard on the band. The biggest problem was Kurt Cobain's drug addiction. Although their next album, *In Utero*, also hit #1 on

the Billboard chart, Kurt Cobain took his own
life just a few months later. It was the sad end of
an incredibly talented and promising group.

However, another grunge band named Pearl Jam was able to handle their early success and continues to record and tour. Much of their power comes from Eddie Vedder, the lead singer. He has a forceful baritone voice that he can make pulse or vibrate. Nobody else sounds like him.

"Post-grunge" or "alternative" rock rose as grunge faded in the mid-'90s. Some alternative bands influenced by grunge include Bush, the Smashing Pumpkins, and Garbage. Another band, the Foo Fighters, was founded in 1994 by Dave Grohl, the former drummer for Nirvana. Many bands from this era, including the Foo Fighters, continue to record music and tour today.

I Want My MTV

MUSIC TELEVISION®

In August 1981, a new and different TV channel appeared on screens across the United States. It was called MTV (Music Television). All it aired was rock music videos. A music video is a short film that promotes a musician or band's song. It was a powerful way for groups to reach a huge audience. That's if their songs were played in heavy rotation. ("Heavy rotation" means the video was on a lot.)

The rock group KISS was played in heavy rotation on MTV. They looked different from any other band. The four members dressed in black leather and wore incredibly high platform shoes. But what really made them stand out was the thick white makeup and designs on their faces. Their signature song was

"Rock and Roll All Nite." The video of KISS performing it nearly always pops up on any list of the ten best videos.

CHAPTER 9
The King of Pop

Early MTV stars included the rock groups Guns N' Roses, Bon Jovi, and Aerosmith, and pop stars Cyndi Lauper and Madonna. What was one thing that all these performers had in common?

Madonna

They were white.

The first few years of MTV programming featured almost no black musicians. Not even Michael Jackson. He was no longer in the Jackson 5 and was working as a solo performer. He had just produced a fantastic video to promote his song "Billie Jean." MTV was not interested in it.

But that was about to change.

Why did MTV air so few videos starring African Americans? David Bowie asked this question while being interviewed on MTV. The answer was that MTV didn't want to "scare" viewers in small towns by showing a "string of . . . black faces, black music."

This was the same sort of racism as in the 1950s when radio stations in white areas had kept rhythm-and-blues music off the air.

The president of CBS Records heard about MTV's refusal to show Michael Jackson videos. (CBS was Michael Jackson's record company.) He got very, very angry and threatened to pull all videos with CBS performers from MTV and go public with MTV's racism.

MTV quickly put the "Billie Jean" video into heavy rotation. They also began airing other African American performers, like Prince.

The "Billie Jean" video was a huge success. The song was on Michael Jackson's *Thriller* album, which has sold one hundred million copies. The "Billie Jean" video certainly helped sales.

A few months later, the thirteen-minute-long video for Michael Jackson's song "Thriller" came out. It was like a short movie. There has really

never been anything to match it. Ever.

A horror-movie director named John Landis created it with Michael. In it, Michael and his date are chased by zombies into an old abandoned house. Michael becomes a zombie himself, and is just about to turn his girlfriend into a zombie, when she wakes up. It's all been a bad dream.

The high point of "Thriller" comes during an amazing dance number. Michael changes into a zombie and then back into a human.

The *Thriller* album also stands as the high point of Michael Jackson's career. He had now earned the title, the King of Pop. Twelve of his singles reached #1 in the United States. In 2001, he was inducted into the Rock and Roll Hall of Fame. During his career, he earned half a billion dollars.

Michael Jackson's private life, however, was strange and lonely. His reputation was scarred by scandals. He was also addicted to a powerful drug that he used to get to sleep. He was rehearsing for a new tour when, on June 25, 2009, he died of an overdose. It was a terrible blow to his millions of fans. "Music has been my outlet, my gift to all the lovers of the world," he said in a 2007 interview. Then he added, "Through it, my music, I know I will live forever." That is certainly true.

Rock and Roll Hall of Fame

Just as there is the Baseball Hall of Fame, there is also a Rock and Roll Hall of Fame. It was created to honor performers, producers, and other important figures who have had a major influence in the music industry, especially in the area of rock and roll.

The first set of performers were inducted in a formal ceremony in 1986 in New York City. They included Elvis Presley, James Brown, Little Richard,

Buddy Holly

Fats Domino, Ray Charles, Chuck Berry, Sam Cooke, and Buddy Holly. The following year Aretha Franklin became the first woman honoree.

There are rules for who can be nominated. Besides being great at what they do, a person needs to have started in the industry twenty-five years before their nomination.

For the next few years, organizers looked for a permanent home where a museum about rock could be built. Cleveland, Ohio, was eventually chosen, and on September 1, 1995, a crowd of more than ten thousand people attended the museum's official opening. In addition to displaying mementos from Hall of Fame inductees, the museum also covers the entire history of rock and roll.

CHAPTER 10
Into the Future

There is no simple definition for what counts as rock and roll. Music critics will probably never stop arguing about it. A lot of fans simply say that they know it when they hear it.

So what about hip-hop?

While hip-hop artists have been inducted into the Rock and Roll Hall of Fame, some music fans

question whether hip-hop counts as rock. One reason is that often, hip-hop artists do not play musical instruments. Instead, an MC, or rapper, recites clever rhyming lyrics, sometimes very quickly, over a DJ track or a pre-recorded beat.

Others believe that even though hip-hop and rock differ in style and sound, they still share the same youthful spirit. And, eventually, just as with rock and roll, hip-hop artists began using their music to address bigger issues, such as poverty, violence, racism, and politics. Groups like Public Enemy and NWA, and solo artists like KRS-One and Ice-T, were revolutionary, because they confronted and exposed problems people were facing in poor urban communities.

Ice-T

Run DMC Meets Aerosmith

In 1975, Steven Tyler and Joe Perry of the rock group Aerosmith wrote the hit song "Walk This Way." Ten years later, Run DMC recorded a cover of it. None of the members of Run DMC had ever heard of the song or of Aerosmith before. It was their producer who persuaded them to do it.

Steven Tyler and Joe Perry played on the Run DMC cover. The video, featuring Run DMC, Tyler, and Perry, cleverly begins with each band playing their version of the song in studios next to each other. Eventually the wall comes down and all the singers perform together for a rock audience. The Run DMC version of "Walk This Way" went higher on record charts than the original.

It was a breakthrough hit for Run DMC. It also proved that hip-hop and rock shared much in common.

Rock began as music made by kids and listened to by kids. Every day, there are young musicians rehearsing in garages, basements, living rooms, and any other place where four or five can get together and practice.

But now members of some rock-and-roll bands, like the Rolling Stones, are all in their seventies. So does rock still hold its appeal?

Every few years, articles in music magazines appear saying that rock is dead. And indeed, many of the biggest and most talented performers today—Beyoncé, Lady Gaga, Taylor Swift—aren't rock stars in the same way Janis Joplin and Jimi Hendrix were.

Beyoncé

There are exciting bands like Vampire Weekend and Arcade Fire creating really interesting rock music. But there is no new rock phenomenon today—no singer or group—that has grabbed hold of the whole world's attention the way the Beatles did.

In his autobiography, *Born to Run*, Bruce Springsteen talks about never imagining he would become a rock legend. He recalls one of the most magical moments in his long career. It was in 1988, when he was onstage performing with many other rock-and-roll musicians. Bruce looked to one side and saw Mick Jagger singing. On his other side was George Harrison of the Beatles playing. Bruce thought about the odds of a pimply kid from Freehold, New Jersey, ending up onstage with his heroes. But it had happened. He was a superstar, too.

This, he thought, was the miracle of rock and roll.

Timeline of Rock and Roll

1877 — Thomas Alva Edison invents the phonograph, which plays recorded music

1952 — Big Mama Thornton records "Hound Dog"

1956 — Elvis Presley appears on *The Ed Sullivan Show*

1959 — Berry Gordy opens Motown Records in Detroit, Michigan

1961 — The Beach Boys are formed

— "Please Mister Postman" by the Marvelettes becomes the first Motown single to reach number one

1964 — The Beatles appear on *The Ed Sullivan Show*

1966 — The Beach Boys release *Pet Sounds*

1967 — The Beatles release *Sgt. Pepper's Lonely Hearts Club Band*

1969 — Woodstock rock music festival is held in upstate New York

1972 — David Bowie releases his glam-rock concept album *The Rise and Fall of Ziggy Stardust and His Spiders from Mars*

1973 — CBGB opens in New York City, hosts punk-rock acts like the Ramones and Blondie

1974 — Bruce Springsteen and the E Street Band first perform

1981 — MTV (Music Television) is launched

1991 — Nirvana releases their album *Nevermind*; grunge rock explodes

2016 — David Bowie dies

2017 — Chuck Berry dies

Timeline of the World

1873	Blue jeans first produced by the Levi-Strauss Company
1955	Disneyland opens
1963	Martin Luther King Jr. gives his "I Have a Dream" speech at a civil rights march in Washington, DC
1964	IBM introduces the first mainframe computer
1966	Pampers disposable diapers become popular
1969	Astronaut Neil Armstrong becomes the first man to walk on the moon
1976	Steve Jobs and Steve Wozniak start Apple Computers
	First outbreak of the Ebola virus
1990	Introduction of the World Wide Web
1991	The Soviet Union collapses
1998	*Harry Potter and the Sorcerer's Stone* is published
2001	The World Trade Center and the Pentagon are attacked by Al-Qaeda
2007	Apple introduces the iPhone
2008	Barack Obama is elected the first African American president of the United States
2009	For the first time in history, the majority of the world's population live in urban areas
2011	Osama bin Laden, mastermind of 9/11, is killed by Navy SEALs

Bibliography

*Books for young readers

DeCurtis, Anthony, James Henke, Holly George-Warren, and Jim Miller, eds. *The Rolling Stone Illustrated History of Rock and Roll: The Definitive History of the Most Important Artists and Their Music*. New York: Random House, 1992.

*Edgers, Geoff. *Who Were the Beatles?* New York: Grosset & Dunlap, 2006.

George-Warren, Holly, and Patricia Romanowski. *The Rolling Stone Encyclopedia of Rock & Roll*. New York: Fireside, 2005.

Guralnick, Peter. *Sam Phillips—The Man Who Invented Rock and Roll*. New York: Little, Brown, 2015.

Harrison, Olivia, and Mark Holborn. *George Harrison: Living in the Material World*. New York: Harry N. Abrams, 2011.

*Holub, Joan. *What Was Woodstock?* New York: Grosset & Dunlap, 2016.

Marcus, Greil. *Mystery Train—Images of America in Rock and Roll Music*. New York: Plume (Penguin Group), 2015.

*Sabol, Stephanie. *Who Is Bruce Springsteen?* New York: Grosset & Dunlap, 2016.

The History of Rock: A Definitive Guide to Rock, Punk, Metal, and Beyond. New York: Parragon Books, 2012.

Elvis Presley with record producer Sam Phillips, second from the left, at Sun Recording Studios

Big Mama Thornton

The Queen Mother meeting Diana Ross and the Supremes in 1968

James Brown at the Newport Jazz Festival on July 6, 1969

The Jackson Five in 1969

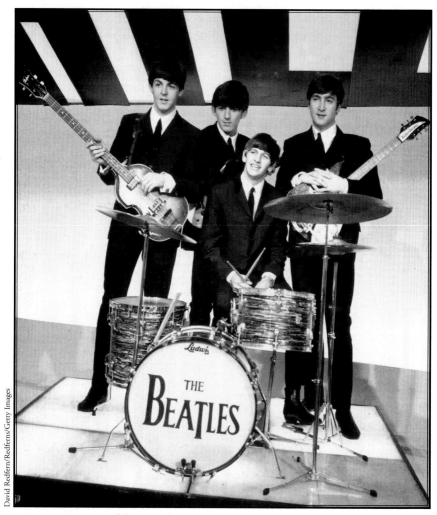

The Beatles in Birmingham, UK, 1963

Police holding back a crowd of Beatles fans

The Beach Boys performing on *The Ed Sullivan Show* in 1964

Big Brother and the Holding Company, including lead singer Janis Joplin

The Beatles at the press launch for their album
Sgt. Pepper's Lonely Hearts Club Band, May 1967

Jimi Hendrix performing at Woodstock, August 18, 1969

Disco star Donna Summer

The Ramones playing at the Palladium in New York, 1978

David Bowie posing as his rock star alter ego Ziggy Stardust

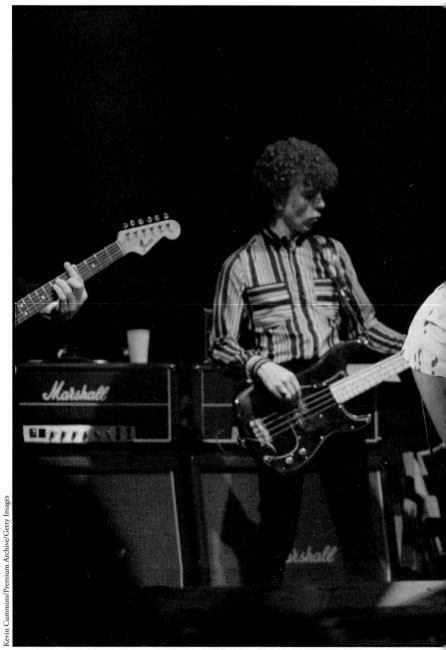

Debbie Harry performing with members of Blondie

The Who in 1975

Bruce Springsteen on the Born in the U.S.A. tour

Michael Jackson on the Bad tour, 1988

Kurt Cobain, singer and guitarist for Nirvana, crowd surfing during a live performance in 1991

Public Enemy on *Saturday Night Live* in 1991

KISS during the closing ceremony of the Winter Olympics
in Salt Lake City, Utah, February 2002

The Rock and Roll Hall of Fame and Museum in Cleveland, Ohio